JUST LOOK AT...

LIFE
IN THE SEA

Bernard Stonehouse

Macdonald Educational

Factual Adviser: Tony Fincham
British Museum (Natural History)

Editor: Nicole Lagneau
Teacher Panel: Deryn Harvey,
Kevin McAlistair, Diane Wilson
Designer: Ewing Paddock
Production: Rosemary Bishop
Picture Research: Peter Harrison

Illustrations
Mike Atkinson 8—9, 12—13, 28—29, 36—37, 40
Ann Baum/Linda Rogers Associates 14—15,
20—21, 34—35, 38—39
Andrew Miller/Artists Partners 17, 18—19, 26—27,
28—29, 30—31
Francis Mosley Cover cartoon, 8, 12, 28, 36, 42

Photographs
Heather Angel/Biofotos, 7, 13, 16, 20, 22BL, 35B
BPCC/Aldus Archive, 27, 39, 43
Robert Harding, 40—41
Eric & David Hosking, 38
Frank Lane Picture Library, 27T
Seaphot, 4—5, 11, 14—15, 19, 22R, 23, 29, 31,
32, 33, 35T, 37, front cover
Tony Stone Associates, 25

Title page photo: Grunts in the Bahamas.

How to use this book

Look first in the contents page to see if the subject you want is listed. For instance, if you want to find out about whales, you will find that they are on pages 34 and 35. The word list explains the more difficult terms found in this book. The index will tell you how many times a particular subject is mentioned and whether there is a picture of it.

Life in the Sea is one of a series of books on Natural History. All the books on this subject have a green colour band around the cover. If you want to know more about natural history, look for other books with a green band in the **Just Look At . . .** series.

© Macdonald & Co. (Publishers) Ltd. 1984

First published in Great Britain in 1984
by Macdonald & Co. (Publishers) Ltd.
London & Sydney.

ISBN 0 356 099601
Printed and bound in Great Britain by Purnell & Sons
(Book Production) Ltd., Paulton, nr. Bristol.

Macdonald & Co. (Publishers) Ltd.
Maxwell House, 74 Worship Street, London EC2A 2EN

CONTENTS

Sea and Shore   **8–13**

Flippers On   10–11
Tides   12–13

Life Close to Land   **14–23**

Seaweeds   16–17
Rocky Shores   18–19
Sand and Mud   20–21
Coral Reefs   22–23

The Open Sea   **24–41**

Life at the Surface   26–27
Fishes   28–29
Life at the Bottom   30–31
Fishing   32–33
Whales and Dolphins   34–35
Warm Seas   36–37
Polar seas   38–39
Marine Research   40–41

Books, Places and Events   42–43
Word list and Index   44–45

Tern

SEA AND SHORE

Living on land, we sometimes forget how much of the world is covered by sea. In fact there is far more sea than land, well over twice the area. The deepest sea is much deeper than the tallest mountains are high. In the days of sailing ships it took weeks to cross the Atlantic Ocean, and you could sail the Pacific Ocean for months on end without seeing land.

How many seas and oceans are there? Sailors used to talk of the 'seven seas', but there is really only one enormous stretch of salty water, continuous over the whole Earth between the continents and islands. There are a few small inland seas too, like the Sea of Galilee and the Caspian Sea, cut off from the rest. We name different parts of this great world ocean just to identify them, and to remind us how different some areas are from others. The Red Sea is not really red (though the rocks around its shore are), but it is the warmest and saltiest of all the seas. The White Sea is not really white, except in winter when it freezes over and is snow-covered like the land around it.

Each bit of sea and ocean has its own special character, and each, from the hottest to the coldest, has particular plants and animals living in it. You do not always see them, for many of the plants are no bigger than a pin-head, and the animals may be transparent, or coloured in such a way that they are hard to find.

◄ All life is said to have begun in the sea. Some of the most interesting and exciting creatures in the world still live there today.

Sea birds, dolphins and flying fish are just three of hundreds of different sea creatures.

Frigate bird

Brown booby

Dolphins

Flying fish

Flippers On

The sea is restless, and changing all the time. Winds raise waves on the surface, and the waves beat against the land, carving out cliffs and beaches. Sun and Moon tug at the sea, causing the tides that expose and cover the shore alternately every day. So the sea is a lively place to live.

In the sea

We cannot live long in the sea. It is too wet for our skins, often too cold, and too salty for us to drink. We cannot see properly under water, or breathe without schnorkels or air bottles to help us. Plants and animals that live in the sea are specially suited for it, often so well suited that they cannot live anywhere else, even in fresh water. But we can find out much about the sea by paddling close to the shore.

We can find out even more about the sea if we can swim just beyond the surf on a calm day and look down into the water through goggles or a face mask. If we dive down a metre or two like a seal or fish and poke about among the seaweeds, we can really begin to feel what it is like to live in the sea.

Living and breathing

Living in sea water is very different from living in air. Sea water supports us and makes us feel weightless. We float if we are breathing normally, but sink if our lungs are empty. Flippers help us to push through the water, like the tail of a fish or the flippers of a seal or penguin. We can breathe through a schnorkel or tube close to the surface.

It is easier to swim underwater with flippers, and goggles help us to see more clearly. But, however hard we try, we shall never be as good as even the smallest fish or crab, so we have to be careful. ▶

Never on your own
Swim only when friends or family are with you, never by yourself. The sea can be dangerous as well as interesting, and even strong swimmers may easily run into difficulties, especially if they stay too long in water and get cold.

Diving

Below two or three metres, the weight of water on our chest compresses our lungs and we are unable to breathe. That is why a diver has to breathe special air, called compressed air. Old-fashioned diving suits had air pumped down to them. Modern divers carry steel bottles of air down with them. Submarines, and diving craft that work at great depths, like *Alvin* in the picture below, need strong steel walls to stand up to the great pressure of water. They too carry their own air supply.

Seeing and hearing

Your eyes cannot focus with sea water against them. That is why goggles or a mask with air inside help you to see more clearly. Daylight penetrates only a few dozen metres into clear water and much less into cloudy water, so it soon becomes dark.

At 100 metres down you need a strong torch to see with, even at mid-day, and *Alvin* carries powerful floodlights to work deep down. Sound carries better in water than in air. We do not hear clearly in the shallows because sounds come at us from all sides, and the surf and pebbles rubbing together are very noisy. Many marine animals, whales, for example rely on sounds much more than sight for finding each other, keeping together and hunting their prey.

▲ This diver is exploring a coral reef. As he is swimming so deep under water, he needs air bottles for breathing and weights to hold him down.

Alvin is a tiny submarine ▶ that takes scientists to explore some of the deepest parts of the sea. It has special claws which can grab rocks or pick up unusual creatures.

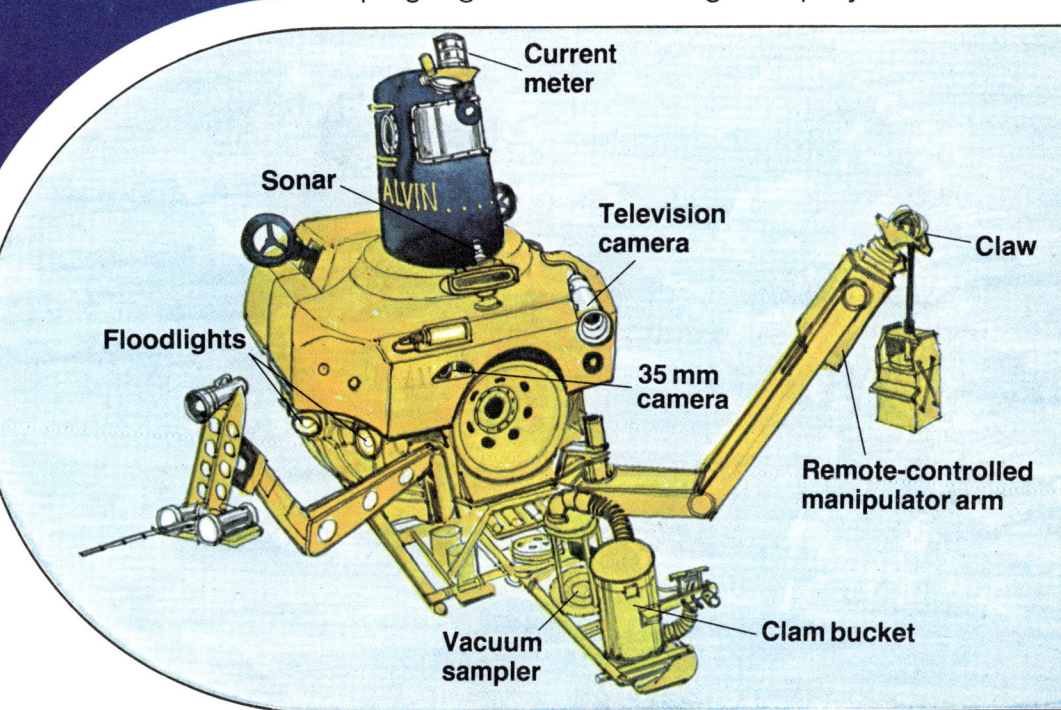

Current meter

Sonar

Television camera

Claw

Floodlights

35 mm camera

Remote-controlled manipulator arm

Vacuum sampler

Clam bucket

Tides

Is the tide in or out? It makes a lot of difference to what you see when you walk along the shore. Tides are controlled by the Sun and Moon, especially the Moon. Twice each day the sea rises high up the shore. The highest point it reaches is called the 'high tide mark'. Twice each day it goes down, leaving a broad band of shore exposed to the air. The lowest point, reached five to six hours after high tide, is the 'low tide mark'.

Walk along the shore at low tide and you will see many plants and animals left behind on the sand after the water has moved out. They live between the high and low tide marks, in the intertidal zone. This is a good time to study them without having to get wet.

Spring tides

Twice a month, two or three days after full Moon and new Moon, high and low tide marks are farthest apart. The high tides are higher than usual and the low tides lower. These are called 'spring tides'. They have nothing to do with the seasons, but occur when the pull from the Moon is strongest.

At a low spring tide you can walk further down the shore than at any other time. This is the best time to see the lowest zones of seaweed and some of the animals that live among them.

Limpets cannot easily hide themselves. They protect themselves from danger by clamping their shells down into the groove they make in the rock. ▼

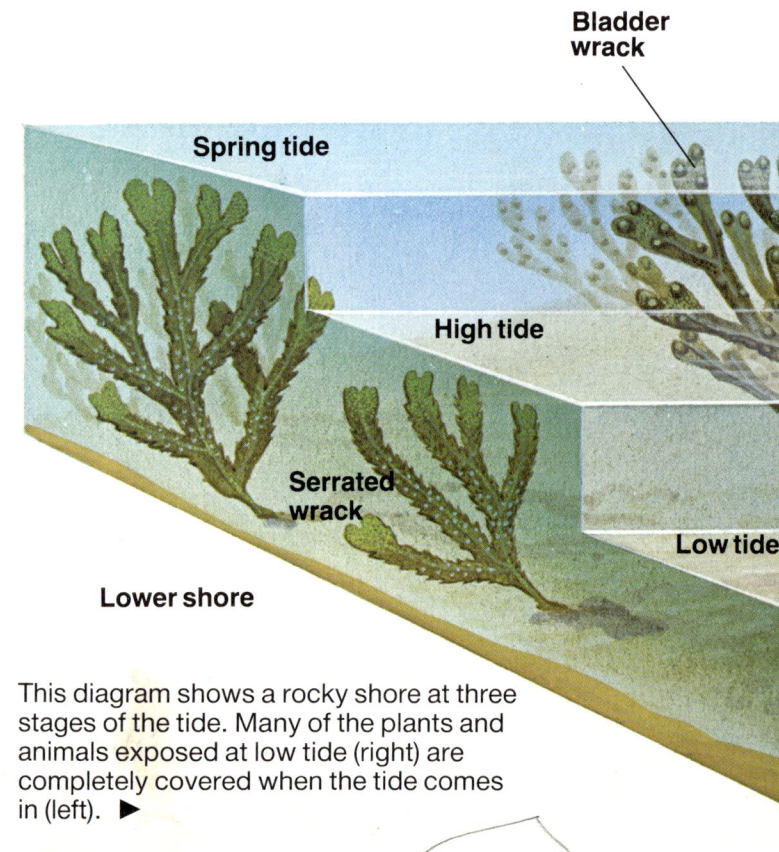

Bladder wrack

Spring tide

High tide

Low tide

Serrated wrack

Lower shore

This diagram shows a rocky shore at three stages of the tide. Many of the plants and animals exposed at low tide (right) are completely covered when the tide comes in (left). ▶

In rough weather the ▶
seas break right over these
headlands and stacks,
carving arches and caves
from the solid rocks.

Erosion

Rough seas pound the coast, especially in
autumn and spring when the gales blow hardest.
They are powerful enough to carve away the
toughest rocks, cutting arches and caves,
undercutting cliffs and causing them to collapse
into the sea. Yet some shore plants and animals
that live between the high and low tide marks are
still able to live even in places like these, clinging
tightly to the rocks even in the worst weather.
The illustration below shows where different
plants and animals live on the splash zone, upper,
middle and lower shores.

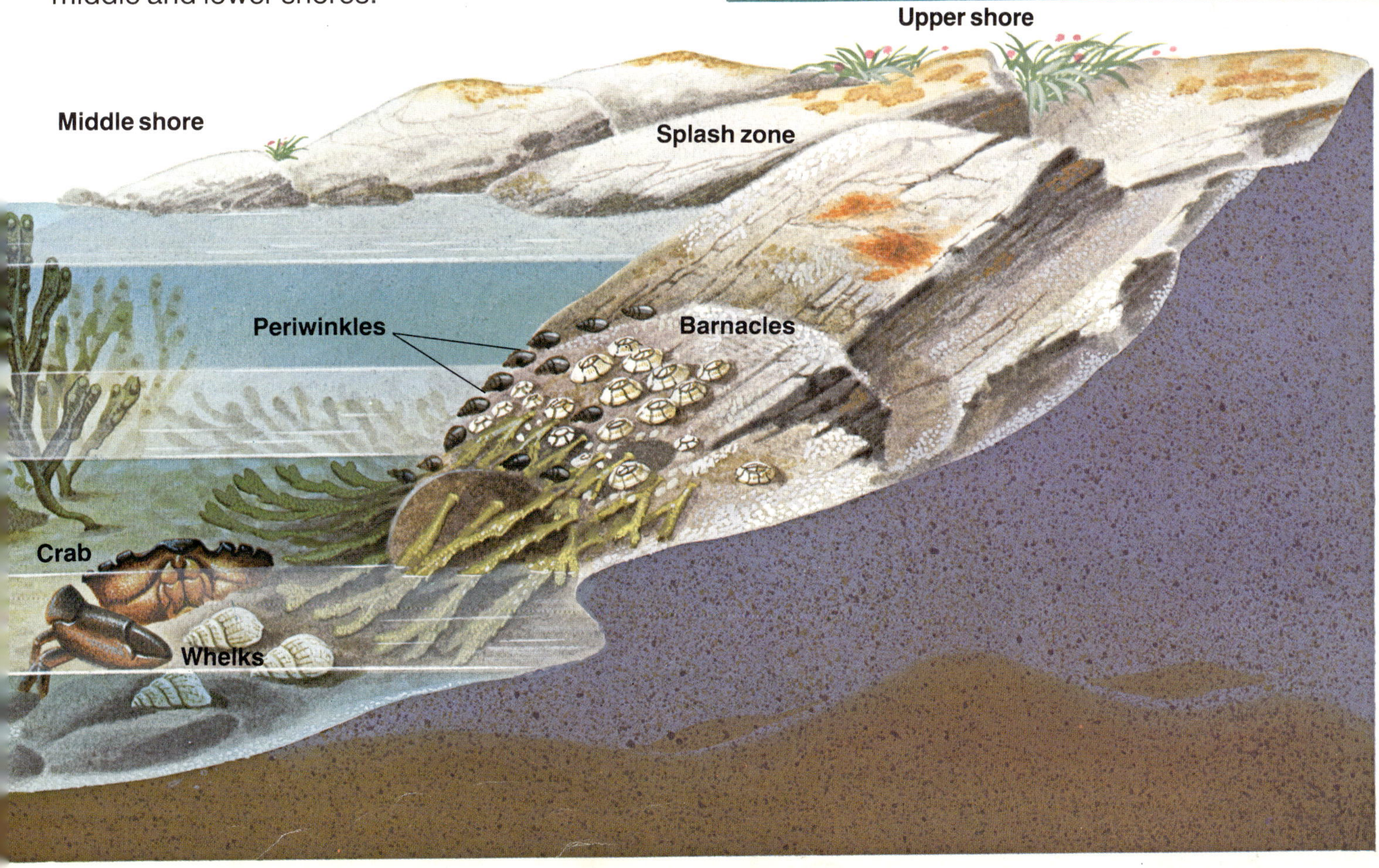

Upper shore

Middle shore

Splash zone

Periwinkles

Barnacles

Crab

Whelks

A river mouth on the coast of Wales, showing different kinds of shore. The dark band along the base of the cliffs and over the rocks is seaweed, exposed because the tide is low.

LIFE CLOSE TO LAND

Here along the shore, at the very edge of the sea, land and water meet. Because the shore is dry at low tide and covered by the sea when the tide is in, it is difficult for plants and animals to settle here. Think of limpets and sea snails living among the rocks half way down this shore. While the tide is in, they are marine animals moving, breathing and feeding under water. This is when they are most active. When the tide goes out, twice daily for several hours at a time, they are left high and dry. They just have to wait, usually in a damp corner among the rocks or under the seaweeds where there is shade and shelter for them. The higher up the shore they live, the longer their wait for the sea to return.

Rocky shores are the best places to live for many organisms. They are firm enough to give footholds for them to cling to, cracks to hide in and weeds to shelter among. Muddy shores and sandy shores are next best. Here you find fewer seaweeds and clinging animals. There are more animals that can burrow and dig into the surface. Pebble shores with loose stones are the most difficult to settle in, because the pebbles roll around with each wave. There are examples of all these kinds of shore in this picture.

An outline of the coast showing muddy shores, rocky shores and sandy shores. ▼

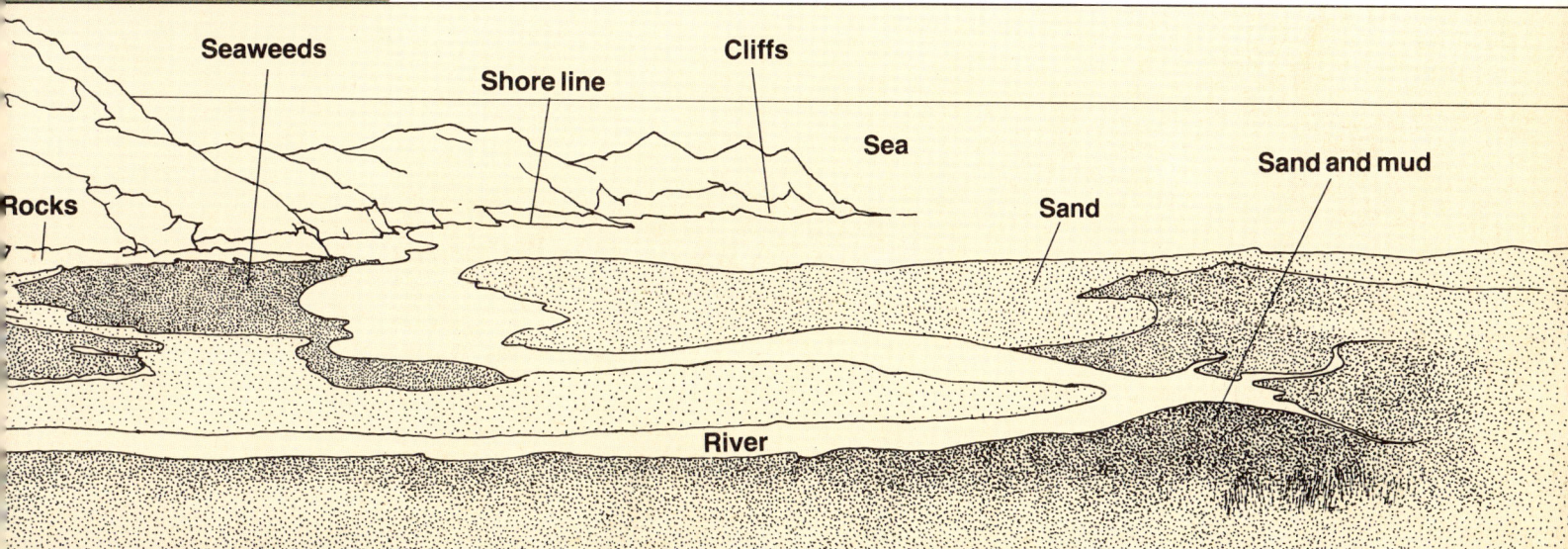

Seaweeds

Shore line

Cliffs

Sea

Sand and mud

Rocks

Sand

River

Seaweeds

Go down to a rocky shore at low tide and see the tangle of red, brown and black seaweeds. You may not notice at first, but there is a pattern to their arrangement. Each species or different kind of seaweed lives in a narrow band along the shore. The bands are narrowest along a sea wall or cliff face, but broaden to a zone several metres wide on a sloping shore. Some species live in a band close to the high tide mark, some on the mid-shore, and some you will see only when the tide is out.

Below low tide
Below the low tide mark are the much longer, tougher oarweeds and kelps, some with strands ten or more metres long. These are seldom exposed completely, but you can watch them swirling and twisting as the waves flow through them. The root-like 'holdfasts' that attach them to the rocks are a safe home for dozens of tiny animals, and the fronds themselves support many more.

Forests of the shore
Watch the seaweeds as the tide sweeps back. First they stir, then they lift and float. As the water deepens they turn into a forest of supple, swaying fronds. Just like the forests on shore, they provide home and shelter for other plants and animals.

Though many seaweeds are brown or red, they contain a green pigment as well that is also present in land plants. The green pigment catches the energy of sunlight and uses it to build up sugars, starches, oils and proteins for the seaweed's own use.

Diatoms
Seaweeds are not the main food of the animals that live on rocky shores, though they are plentiful on this kind of shore. Far more important are the much smaller single-celled plants called diatoms. They live on surfaces and form a slippery green film over the rocks. These too catch sunlight, whether on the rock or weed surfaces, or floating free in the water. They are also the main food of browsing animals.

This hold-fast of a large ▶ seaweed is firmly attached to rocks at the low tide mark. It is a safe home for dozens of tiny animals.

Channelled wrack

Spiral wrack

Bladder wrack

Serrated wrack

Oarweed

Red seaweed

◄ These brown seaweeds all live in narrow bands along the shore. Channelled wrack is found just below the high water mark. In hot weather it may dry out completely between tides and turn black.

◄ Spiral wrack is found further down the shore and marks the lower edge of the upper shore. Lower still you will find a greeny-brown weed called bladder wrack, which you can pop between your fingers. Below this is serrated wrack. This has saw-like edges and is exposed for just an hour or two at low water.

◄ Below the low tide mark, tough oarweeds can be seen, swirling and twisting as the waves flow through them.

◄ Both red and brown seaweeds contain the same green pigment as all other green plants. Red ones live well down the shore below the rest.

Rocky Shores

Small pools among the rocks are places where water remains behind even when the tide has gone out everywhere else. Small ones warm up in the sun and may even dry out. Big ones are much more stable, and often crammed with busy life. You will meet many shore animals there. If you catch them, put them back quickly. They will not be able to live long out of water.

Food chains

Periwinkle snails have curly, twisted shells. Limpets have rounded or conical shells. They both glide over the rocks and seaweeds, feeding by scraping off diatoms. You can sometimes see their trails and the scrape marks left by their tongues. Mussels and barnacles stay fixed to the rocks, but suck sea water into their shells and filter out food particles.

Crabs, prawns, dog-whelks (another kind of sea snail) and starfish hunt actively for larger food. So do hermit crabs, that live in abandoned sea-shells, and many of the little fish you see darting among the weeds. Sea anemones usually stay in one place. They look like lumps of dark red or green jelly when the tide is out, but under water they let out a flower-like circle of tentacles that trap scraps of food. Sea urchins are surprisingly active, going for walks on their spines and chewing up all kinds of food with file-like teeth.

Holding tight

All the creatures of the rocky shore must be firmly anchored or small enough to hide for days when the wind blows and the waves come pounding in. They need to be tough too.

Rock pools are never as crowded as this, ▶ although a large one may contain all these kinds of creatures and more.

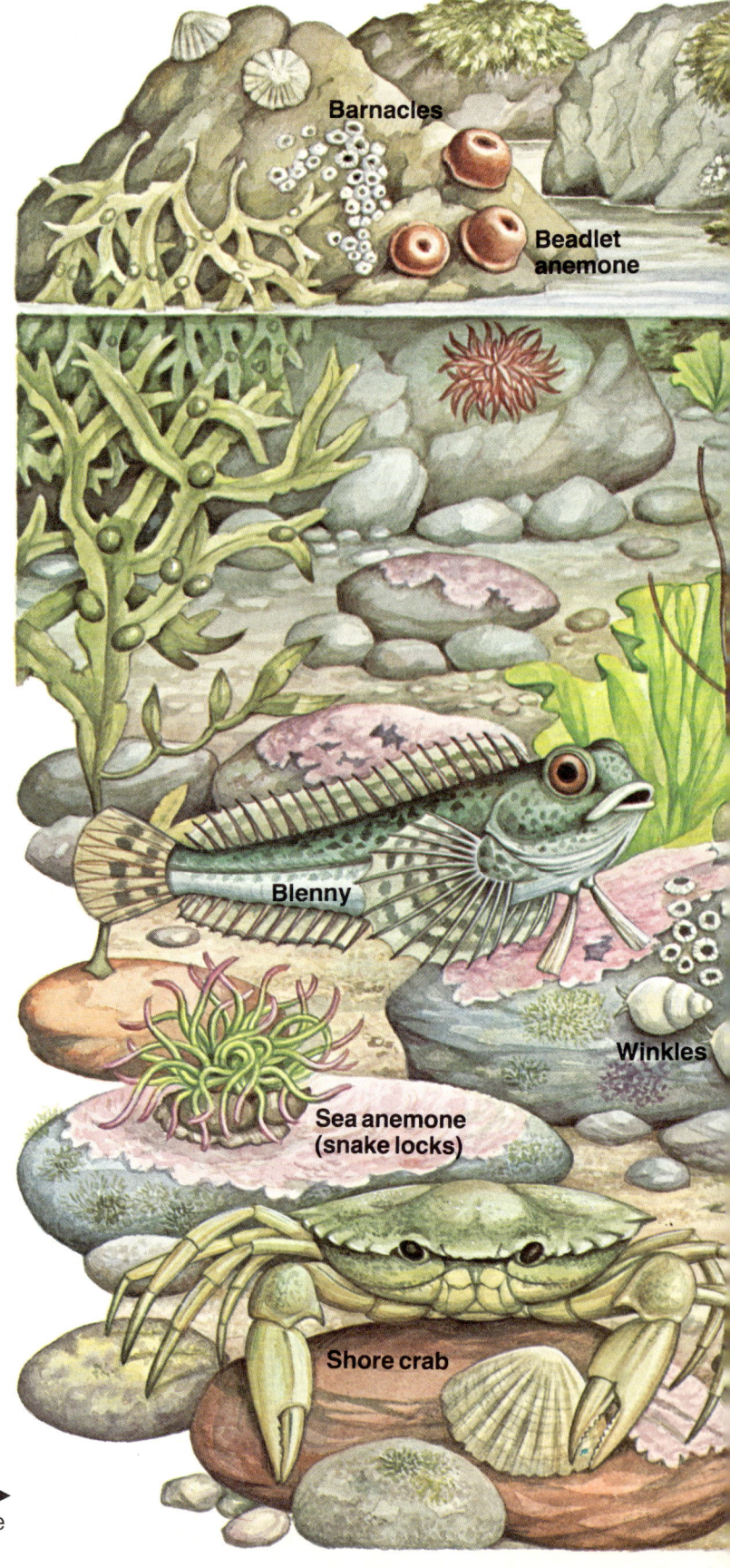

Barnacles

Beadlet anemone

Blenny

Winkles

Sea anemone (snake locks)

Shore crab

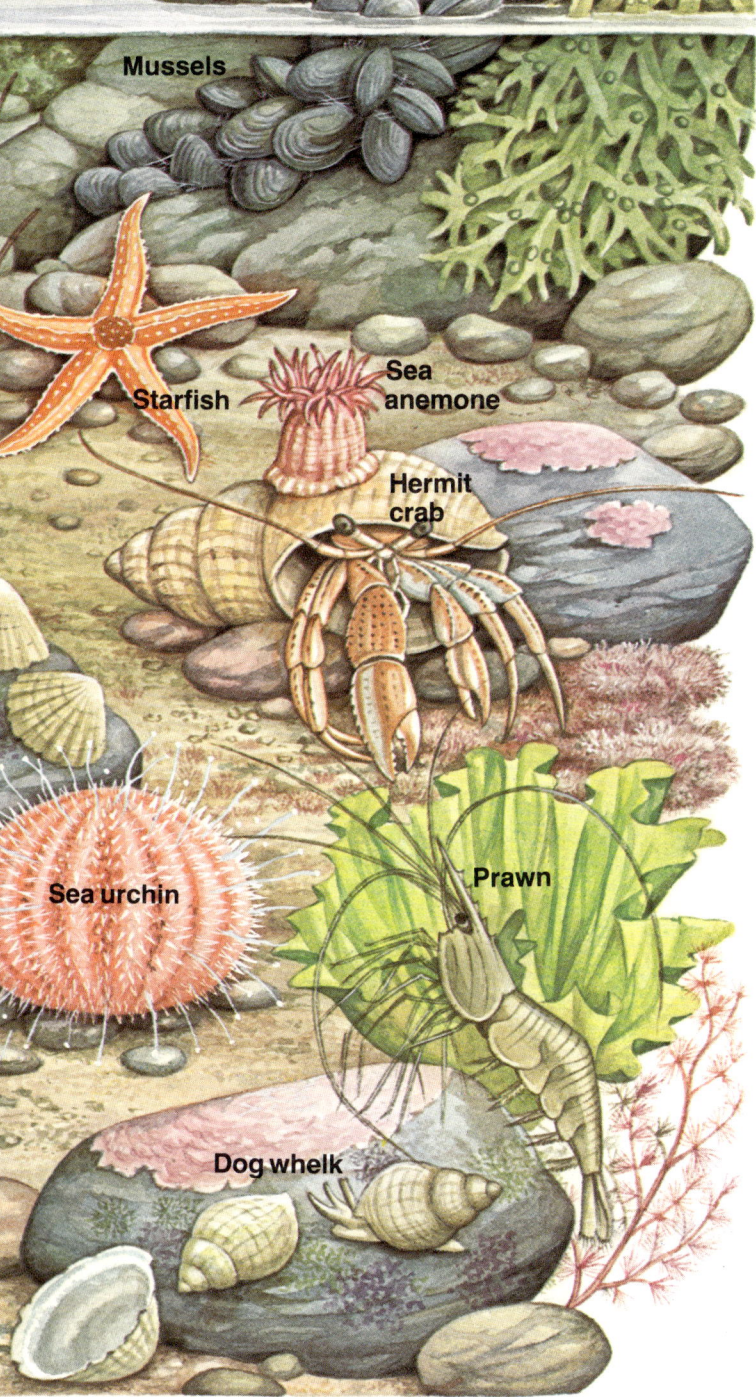

Limpets

Mussels

Starfish

Sea anemone

Hermit crab

Sea urchin

Prawn

Dog whelk

Seaweeds, firmly anchored by their holdfasts, are supple enough to bend and do not tear easily, though you will see plenty of pieces torn off and washed up after a storm. Limpets are thick-shelled and hold on by suction. Try lifting one off the rocks with your fingers and you will see how tightly they grip. Always put them back exactly where you found them.

Barnacles are firmly fixed to the rocks. They relax when the tide comes up, and open the trapdoor in the centre of their hard outer plates to draw in water and food.

Crabs and other mobile animals come out to feed. Periwinkles begin to wander, as soon as the water wets them. You can mark snails, limpets or crabs with a dash of quick-drying paint (nail varnish works well), and often find the same ones in the same places day after day.

▲ A typical rocky shore. The outgoing tide exposes the brown algae growing among heavy boulders at the foot of the cliff.

Sand and Mud

Sand is coarsely-ground rock particles. Mud is more finely ground, with particles so small that they hold water between them and turn into a slippery, gooey mass. Often the two are mixed. Sandy and muddy shores may be too soft for seaweeds to attach themselves to, but sea grasses and some other salt-loving plants settle on them, and many small animals prefer them to hard rock surfaces.

Digging and burrowing

Mixtures of sand and mud provide some of the richest shore habitats. Most animals that live on sandy and muddy shores live under the sand as there is nothing for them to cling to on the surface. Sand is moved easily by wind and waves so most animals, such as lug-worms, shrimps, cockles and razor shells dig themselves into the sand or mud. There they are well protected from the waves at high tide but the sand stays firm and damp at low tide.

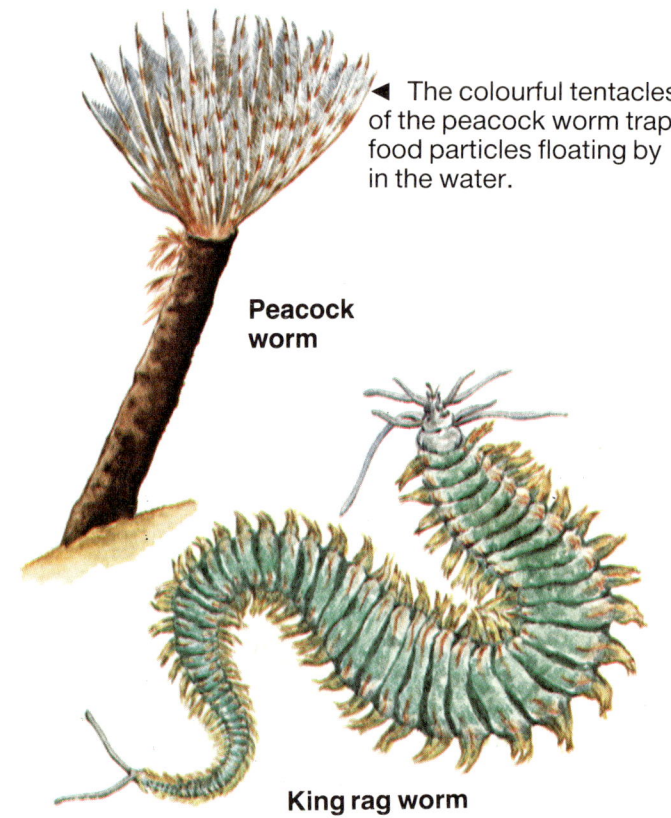

◀ The colourful tentacles of the peacock worm trap food particles floating by in the water.

Peacock worm

King rag worm

▲ Rag worms wriggle over the surface on long bristly legs, the tentacles on the head help them to find their prey.

◀ Ghost crabs are sand-coloured. If they stay in the same spot without moving for long they seem to melt away into the sand.

Curlews

Oyster catchers

Periwinkles

Cockles

Lugworm casts

Hermit crab

Scallops

▲ Dozens of different animals are found on the surface of the sandy mud, whilst others, like cockles and lugworms, burrow just below.

Each animal has adapted to the place where it lives. Sand animals have filters to keep sand out of their breathing tubes for instance. Fan worms live in tubes of sand. They spread a net of colourful tentacles to trap the food particles floating in the water. They are themselves food for browsing fish, but can pull back quickly into their tubes if danger threatens.

Lugworms eat the sand and digest the food particles, leaving worm casts of indigestible sand grains. They too live in tubes, and rely on the fresh supply of food brought to their doorstep by each new tide. Rag worms wriggle over the surface on long bristly legs, poking out a fleshy tube armed with teeth and jaws. Cockles, oysters, mussels, razor shells and other shell-fish open their shells and draw in streams of water, filtering out the diatoms and food debris and at the same time taking the oxygen they need from the water.

Waders
Muddy estuaries and shores are popular feeding grounds for birds, especially long-legged wading birds like oyster-catchers, curlew, dunlin and red shank, that gather in their thousands to feed at low tide. They catch most of their food at the water's edge, digging in the mud with their long bills to haul out worms and shell-fish.

Coral Reefs

Coral is made by tiny animals like pinhead-sized sea anemones called polyps. They make little tubes and platforms of horn or chalky stone for themselves. They live in all seas from the coldest to the warmest, but the ones forming coral reefs are found in warm tropical waters.

There are many different kinds of coral polyps, but they mostly work together, building up sticks, branches and blocks of the stony material we call coral. Billions and billions of them together, working in warm seas, build up huge reefs or banks of coral big enough to encircle whole islands. The Great Barrier Reef of eastern Australia, the world's biggest coral reef, is nearly 2,000 km long and in places over 100 km wide.

Coral animals contain green plant cells that exchange food and gases with them, so they work best in clear, shallow water where sunlight can reach them. Coral reefs are lively, colourful places. The coral itself may be pink, blue or white, but even more brilliant are the sponges, shell-fish, shrimps and vividly-coloured fish that lurk among the reefs.

◄ This crown-of-thorns starfish browses on a coral reef, killing and eating the polyps that form it. Starfish can cause severe damage to reefs.

▲ Many brightly coloured fish, like these blue grunts, feed among the coral reefs, nibbling the surface with razor-sharp front teeth.

Glass-bottomed boats

You can sometimes walk on a coral reef at low tide. If you do, take care not to stub your toes on the hard spikes of coral, or stand on the poisonous fish you sometimes find there, or catch your foot in giant clams, that may close like a rat-trap.

A safer and better way is to drift over the reef in a glass-bottomed boat. It lets you see everything going on below with the least possible disturbance. Now you can see the millions of tiny fish browsing on the coral walls, the orange and yellow sponges, the curious shapes — fans

▲ A diver examining by floodlight some of the vividly coloured corals making up the reef. Under natural light, all their bright colours would disappear.

stag-horns, mushrooms and brain-like shapes — made up of different coral species. You may have to look carefully to see the lovely shells, the elegant, long-limbed shrimps and brilliant sea slugs because their colours blend well with the background. You might see dark sea urchins, each with a tiny golden fish living among its knitting-needle spines. And watch out for speckled moray eels, that wind among the corals and snap at your hand or anything that moves.

THE OPEN SEA

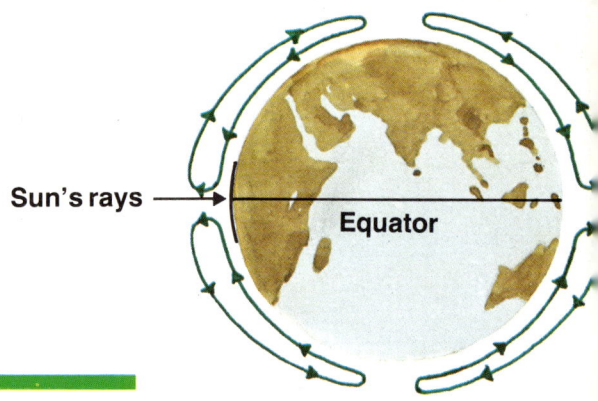

Sun's rays → Equator

Close to the shore the sea is brown or green, because of the mud washed down from the land and the tiny green plants that swarm in it. Open oceans, out of sight of land, are steel grey or blue. To astronauts in outer space the whole Earth looks blue, simply because so much of its surface is blue sea.

The trade winds of the tropics and the westerlies of cooler climates blow constantly around the world. They blow the sea before them, setting up water currents that sweep across the ocean surface like broad rivers. The Gulf Stream brings warm surface water across the Atlantic Ocean. Without it, Britain and Iceland would be very much colder in winter.

Each big ocean has several currents that carry warm equatorial water north and south and cooler waters toward the equator. Other currents circulate deep down. Cold water from melted ice along the shores of Antarctica spreads northward across the bed of the southern Atlantic Ocean as far as the equator and beyond. This is very important for living creatures because some water masses contain more of the nutrients and oxygen that plants and animals need for their survival than others. The currents ensure that there is a constant stirring and mixing of water masses in the oceans. So the richest waters return to the surface for their nutrients to be used.

▲ The sun warms the air most at the equator. The air rises to be replaced by cooler air from temperate regions.

▲ Strong winds push the surface waters of the ocean before them, causing current.

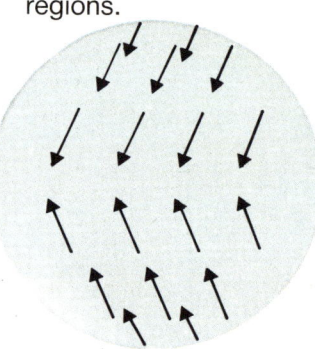

▲ Currents are also caused by the rotation of the Earth, usually clockwise in the northern hemisphere and counter-clockwise in the southern hemisphere.

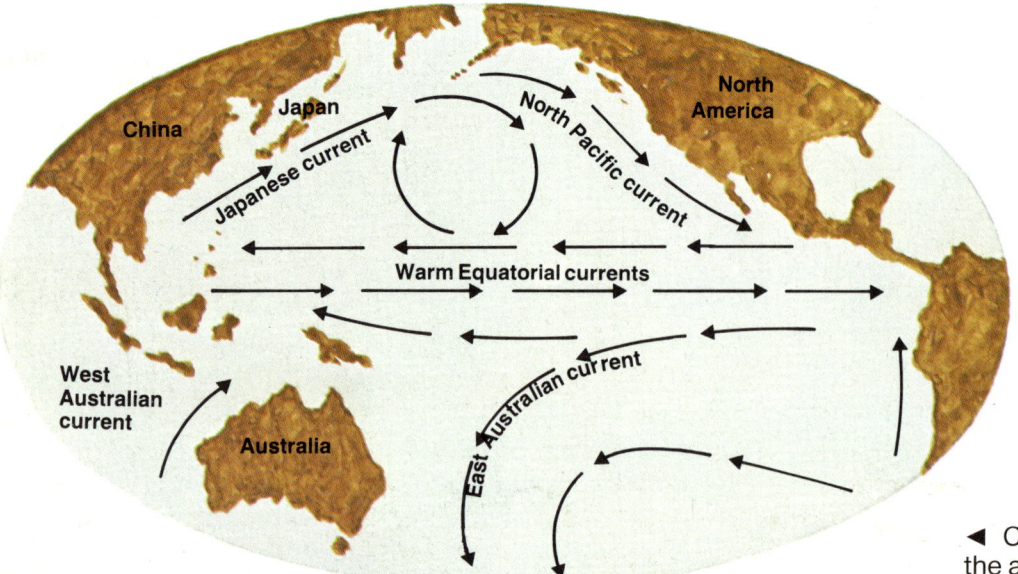

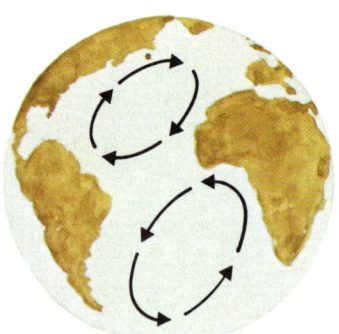

◄ Currents of the Pacific Ocean, shown by the arrows, carry warm water into cold regions, and cold water toward the equator.

Rough seas batter an oil rig. Notice the band of seaweeds growing on the concrete legs of the rig.

Life at the Surface

In the sea, like everywhere else, plants and animals depend on each other for living. Plants absorb energy from sunlight, and minerals and vital gases from the water surrounding them. Like chemical factories, they turn these raw materials into the complex chemicals they need for their own growth and reproduction. Herbivorous animals eat the plants and carnivorous animals eat the herbivores (and each other) to get their share of energy and life-giving nutrients.

Animals put back the minerals they do not use expelling their waste materials into the water, and the plants use them again. Both animals and plants give up more valuable minerals when they die — and so the constant circulation of nutrients continues.

No trees in the sea

The tiny diatoms and other single-celled plants that we meet on the shore are the typical plants of the open ocean. There are many different kinds, with wonderful shapes and patterns on their surface, but they are all small. In the open sea there is nothing so big as even the smallest seaweed.

Why are land plants big and ocean plants small? Each little green cell in the sea has all it needs to grow and reproduce either within itself, or in the sea immediately around it. They do not need roots or shoots, leaves, branches or stems. They divide by splitting, so do not need flowers or seeds. The smaller and simpler they are, the more efficient they can be at their basic jobs of trapping sunlight, absorbing nutrients, and multiplying.

The animals that feed on these plant cells are mostly tiny too. You can often catch them by towing a very fine net through the water.

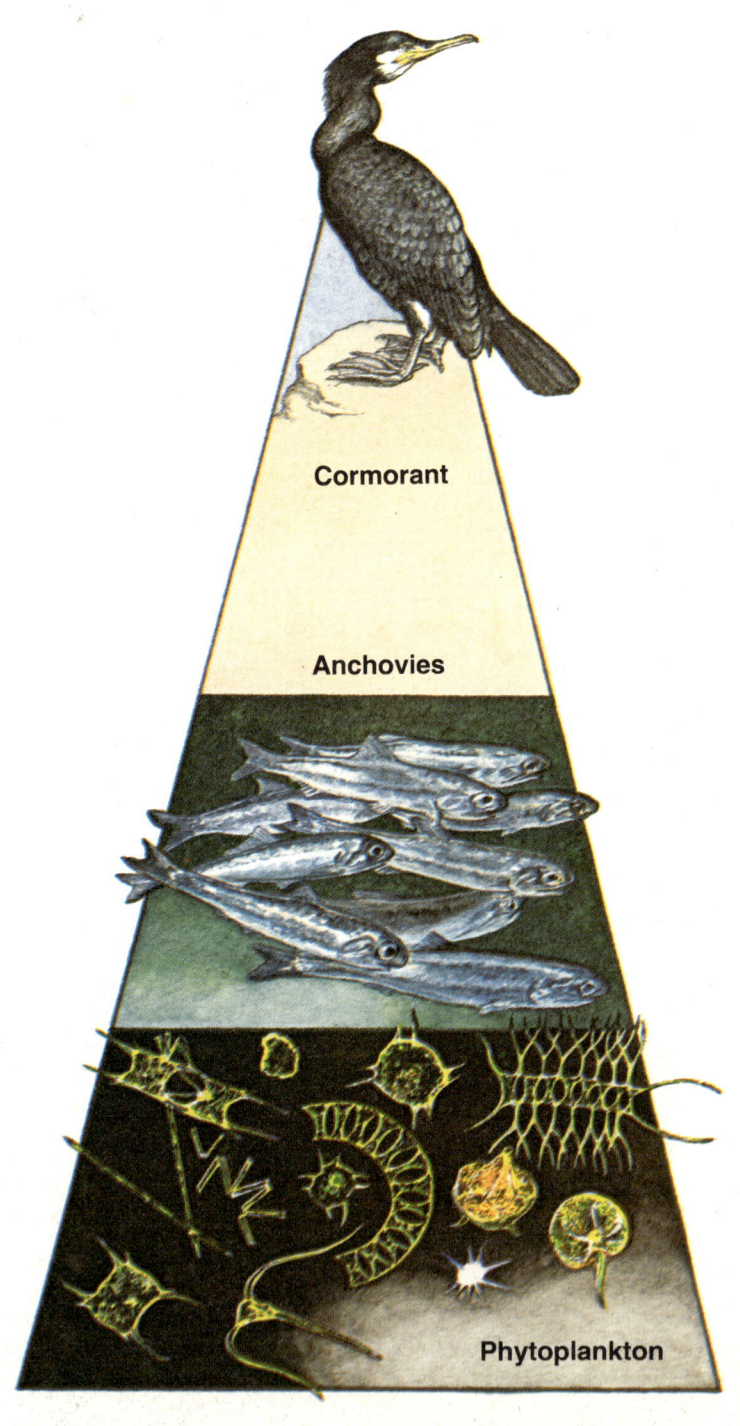

Cormorant

Anchovies

Phytoplankton

▲ It takes millions of the plankton creatures at the bottom of the pyramid to feed the hundreds of fish that one bird eats in a year.

Some of the tiny animals ▶ called zooplankton that float in the surface waters provide food for other animals.

▲ A gannet in a steep dive, about to plunge into the sea to catch a fish.

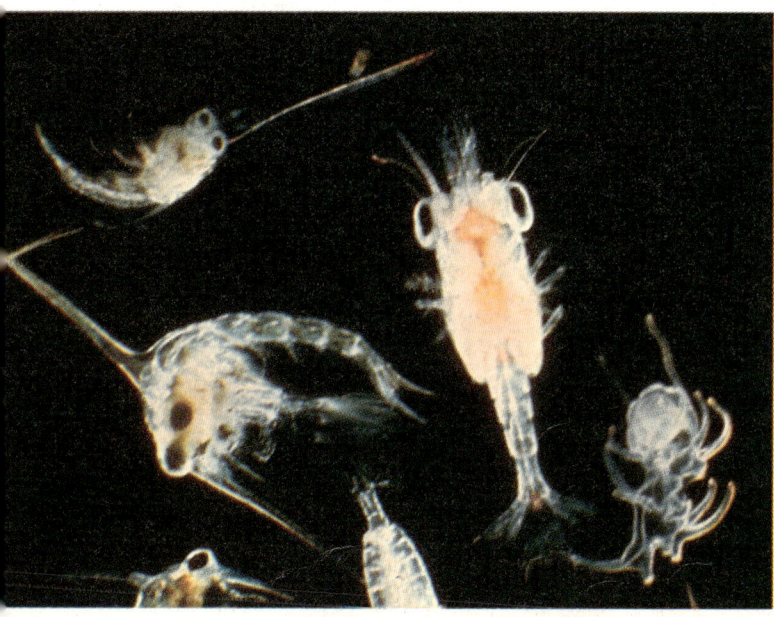

Or you could pour several buckets of clean sea water through the net. You will need a hand lens or microscope to see them properly, for they are mostly less than a centimetre long and some are very much smaller. Biologists call the life at the sea surface 'plankton', which means drifters.

Plankton

Plant drifters (phytoplankton) and animal drifters (zooplankton) often collect at the ocean surface in huge shoals. Zooplankton includes both the tiny animals you catch in a fine net and some much larger ones, like jellyfish. The smaller animals have among them many different kinds or species that live their whole lives in the plankton. Krill, the shrimp-like creatures that many whales feed on, is one example. But they also include many young creatures: larval fish recently hatched from their eggs, and larval forms of crabs, mussels, starfish, sponges, sea anemones and shell-fish. The ocean surface is their nursery, where there is plenty of food for them and room to grow.

Feeding

Each animal has its own way of catching food. Among the herbivores, some have comb-like bristles, others tentacles, nets or simply wide mouths. One way or another they trap and swallow the phytoplankton, which is constantly available for them so long as the growing season lasts. The carnivores, generally larger and more active, include ferocious arrow-worms and large fish larvae, jellyfish and big predatory shrimps.

Many kinds of adult fish too specialize in feeding on the plankton. The smaller ones, like anchovies and herrings, hunt together in shoals of many thousands. Bigger fish like basking sharks, which may be 13 to 15 metres long, drift alone or in groups of five or six. Fish that feed on plankton have networks of bony or gristly spines in their mouths, that let the sea water through but hold back the food particles. Some birds too are plankton-eaters such as, storm petrels, fulmars and several kinds of penguins.

Fishes

The world's smallest fish are only two to three millimetres long, the biggest grow to about 15 metres. In between come fish of all shapes and sizes, from long narrow eels and pipe-fish to fat round sun-fish and puffer-fish. There are fish that fly and fish that walk, fish you can see through, fish with headlamps, mirror scales and rows of lights along their sides, and fish that catch other fish with a rod and line.

Fish live at all depths of the sea. The most brilliantly coloured ones you see generally in the bright, dappled sunlight of coral reefs. Fish of deep water are often black or dark red, but with lights or silvery reflectors that flash as they move. Surface-living fish include long, slender hunters like dolphin-fish, marlin and tuna, that are built for speed. In contrast are plump, lazy sun-fish, basking sharks and black manta rays six to eight metres across, that drift or flap slowly through surface waters munching plankton. Mantas sometimes leap out of the sea, landing with a smack that you can hear very far away. Nobody knows why they do it.

▲ This 'doctor' fish lives by cleaning out the dead skin and food particles from the mouths of larger fish. Sometimes, the larger fish queue up to be cleaned.

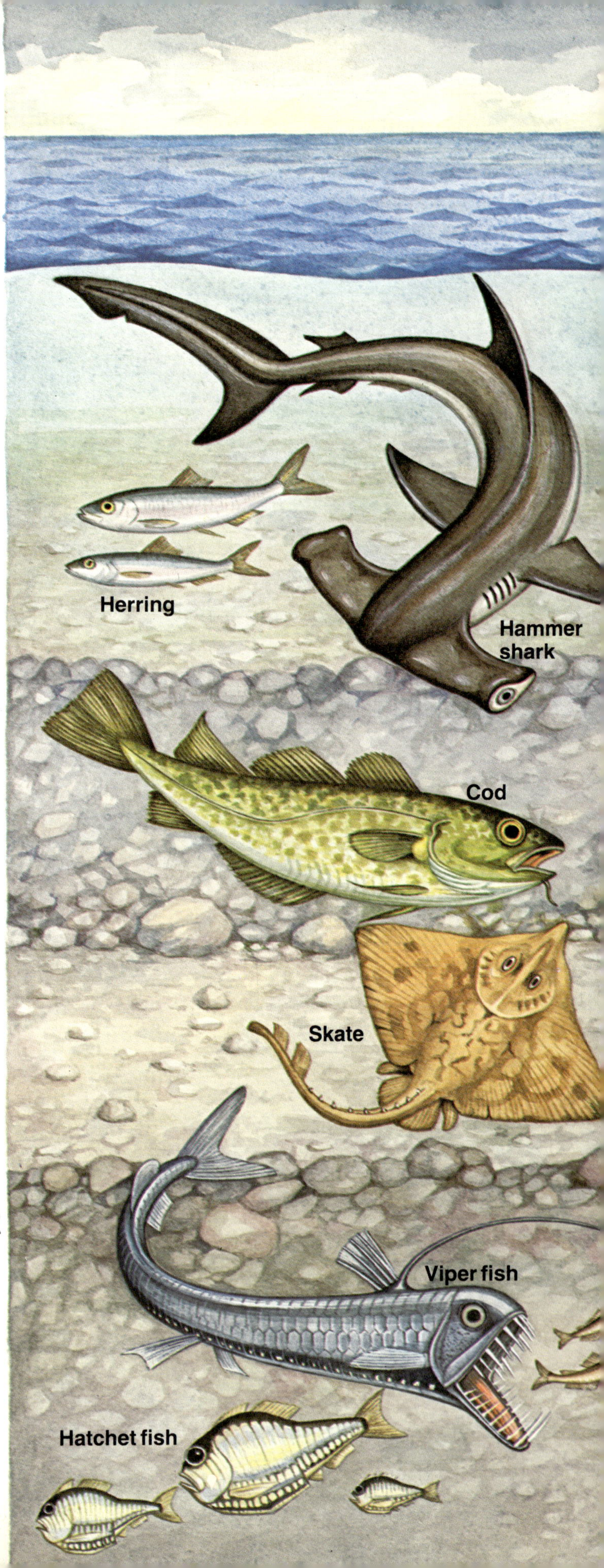

Herring

Hammer shark

Cod

Skate

Viper fish

Hatchet fish

Flying fish

Manta ray

Sun-fish

Mackerel

Tuna

Haddock

Prawn

Angler fish

◄ A selection of fish from all the oceans, crowded together to show some of their strange shapes. Surface-living fish are at the top, shallow water fish below, and deep water fish down at the very bottom.

▲ The huge eyes, gold and silver reflectors and rows of coloured spots help this deep water fish to find others in the dark.

Sharks

Only a few of the biggest fish are dangerous to humans, and then only occasionally. Great white sharks, blue pointers and curiously-shaped hammer-head sharks have all been known to attack people, but we are never more than a snack for a big one. One good-sized shark caught in an Australian harbour had in its stomach eight legs of mutton and 130 kilograms of other meat, as well as half a pig, half a dog and all kinds of rubbish. Today people are still wary of swimming alone off South Africa, Australia and tropical America.

Lanterns

Deep water fish live in permanent, year-round darkness. They probably hunt by sound and scent rather than sight, but need lights to find and identify each other when they come to mating.

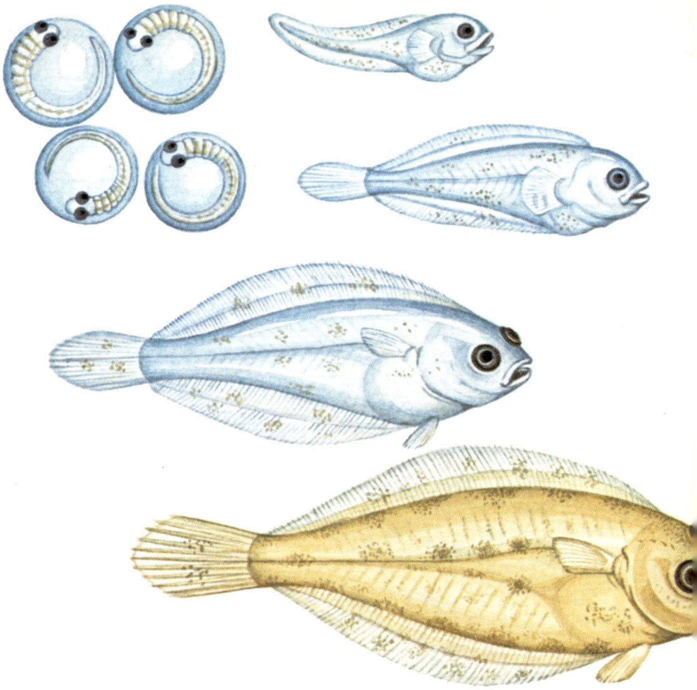

Life at the Bottom

The sea bed starts just below the low tide mark. Like shores it can be rocky, sandy, muddy or a mixture of all three. Walking down through the tangle of kelps and oarweeds we pass first into a zone of rough water. It is difficult to walk or swim straight, or even see properly, because everything is stirred and buffeted by the waves. Then at a depth of about 15 metres the water is suddenly still. It is like being in a huge, dimly-lit room. We cannot quite see the walls, but the floor is carpeted with red and brown seaweeds and the ceiling, the sea surface, billows like a tent above us.

In the shallows

Shoals of little fish dart over the weeds, swimming in formation and dodging down out of sight at the least sign of danger. Among the seaweeds are many of the animals familiar to us from the shore, though many of them are larger.

The crabs, lobsters, starfish, sea urchins and shellfish shown here are some of the wide variety of creatures to be found on the sea bed in shallow water. ▼

Soft coral

Edible crab

Sea urchin

Razor shell

Eyed-finger sponge

Mussel shell

Lobster

Dog whelks

Plaice eggs hatch after three weeks. At first they are like ordinary fish. When the plaice is 40 days old it begins to turn onto its left side and its left eye moves across the skull towards its right eye.

This is where the older, more adult animals live. Big crabs and lobsters, starfish and sea urchins rasp off algae and small animals, with a scattering of sponges, shell-fish, sea slugs, whelks, and ribbon-worms like long, brightly striped bootlaces.

There are bigger fish too: large-mouthed saithe, whiting and cod gulping for shrimps and worms on the sea bed. There are also plaice, and brill — curious flat-fish half-buried in the sand, that flop away like big leaves when we disturb them. These start life like ordinary fish, but change shape during growth so they can still see, breathe and catch prey while lying half-buried.

Deeper water

Going deeper it soon gets dark, even at mid-day, and colour disappears — everything looks greeny-grey. At 100 metres there are no more seaweeds because there is not enough light for them to grow. At this depth and below animals feed mainly on each other and on the debris that sinks slowly down from above.

At 1,000 metres there is no glimmer of light, but there are still plenty of animals, mostly filter-feeding sponges, worms, starfish and shell-fish. These continue right down to the deepest depths we know, over 10,000 metres. There they live in a weird world under immense pressure from the sea, and in inky darkness except for the flashing lights of passing fish, shrimps and squid.

▲ This grey gurnard uses its spiny fin-rays to 'taste' the sand, helping it to find its prey.

Tortoise shell limpets

Starfish

Lump sucker

Fishing

For thousands of years we have been catching fish. The traditional methods of small nets cast from the shore, fish traps, baited hooks and spearing are still used in different parts of the world. But most of the fish we eat today have been caught from big ships in deep water, using nylon nets that take thousands of fish at a time.

Fishing grounds

The best fishing grounds are in cool seas. The North Sea, the North Pacific and Atlantic are good examples where food is plentiful and the fish grow quickly. The best fish to catch are the kinds that live together in big shoals, such as herring, tuna and sardines.

Trawl net

▲ These fishermen of East Africa are carrying their nets down to the sea. Throwing a net from the shore is one of the oldest ways of catching fish.

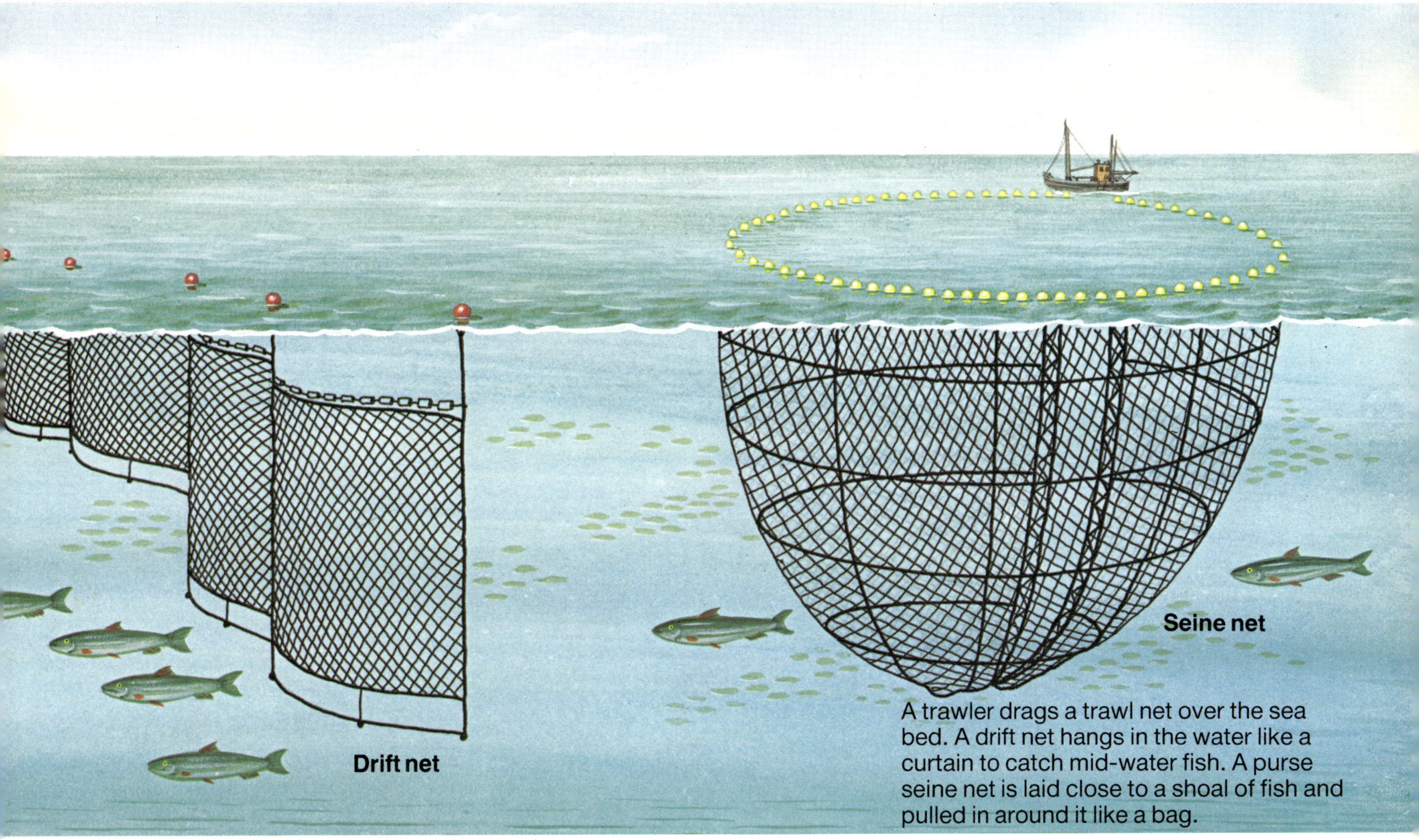

Seine net

Drift net

A trawler drags a trawl net over the sea bed. A drift net hangs in the water like a curtain to catch mid-water fish. A purse seine net is laid close to a shoal of fish and pulled in around it like a bag.

Species found close to the sea bed, like cod, hake, haddock and whiting, are caught in trawls. Trawls are conical nets towed behind powerful trawlers on the end of long steel ropes. Surface-living fish are caught in drift nets or in seine nets. Once caught the fish are brought aboard fish factories, gutted, cleaned, and frozen or packed in ice for the journey to market.

Overfishing

We are so good at catching fish, with our big ships and nets, that we are catching too many. Species like cod, herring and mackerel, that used to be very plentiful and cheap, are now scarce and expensive. Part of the trouble is that we catch many before they have had chance to grow to full size and reproduce.

An alternative method of providing more fish is fish farming. Expensive fish such as trout and salmon are reared in bays and estuaries where they can be looked after, fed, and taken to market as soon as they are big enough. Soon, some of the cheaper fish may be farmed in this way.

▲ Hauling in a trawl net full of fish on a large modern trawler. Pulled quickly through the sea, the trawl net catches many hundreds of fish at a time.

Whales
and Dolphins

Over 30 metres long and weighing 100 tonnes or more, blue whales are the biggest animals in the sea and the biggest in the world. The sperm whale is only half as long and less than half the weight, though still much bigger than the elephant. Whales look like big fish but are mammals — warm-blooded animals like elephants and people. Whales have lungs and so usually they have to swim close to the surface to breathe air. Some like the sperm whale can dive very deep and hold their breath for over an hour.

There are two main kinds of whales. Toothed whales include sperm whales, killer whales and the much smaller porpoises and dolphins. They all have teeth, though some have them only in the lower jaw, some only one on either side, and a few have teeth that never grow at all. Baleen whales include blue whales and all the bigger species.

▲ Elephants are the biggest animals you will find on land. The biggest whales weigh as much as 16—20 elephants. The sperm whale below is only a middle sized whale, about 20 metres long.

▲ Killer whales, up to 10 metres long, are fierce hunters of seals and other whales.

▲ Dolphins are the smallest whales. Some are only 1½—2 metres long.

▲ Whales are sometimes washed up on shore. To save their lives, they have to be shaded from the sun and carried back into the water as soon as possible.

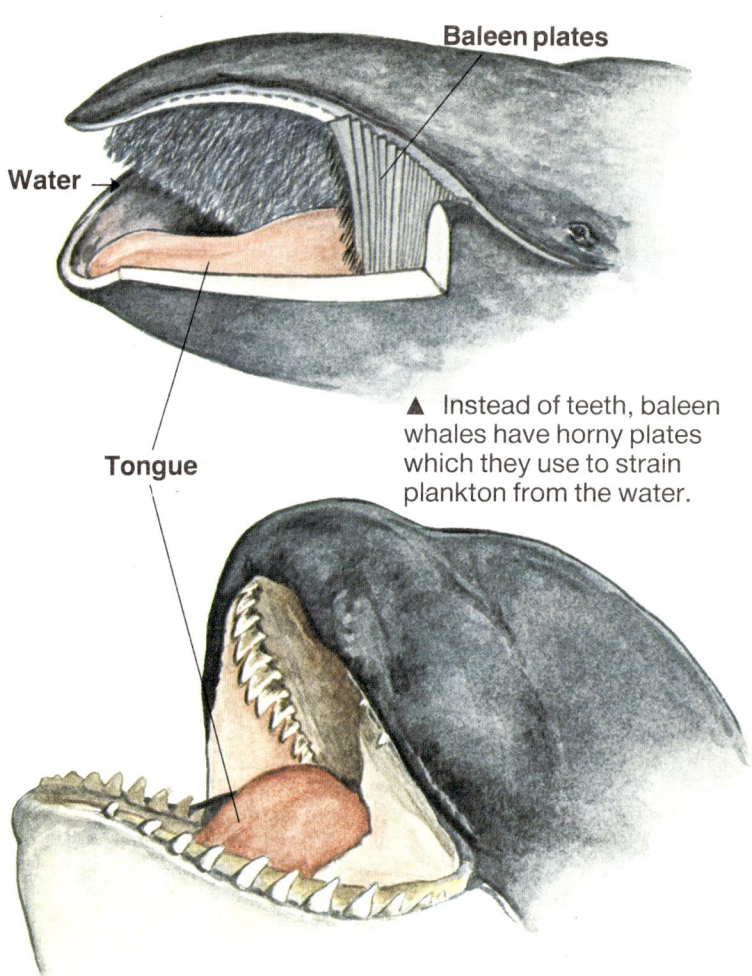

Water →
Baleen plates
Tongue

▲ Instead of teeth, baleen whales have horny plates which they use to strain plankton from the water.

▲ Killer whales hunt together in groups in the cold polar seas. They will attack anything from other whales to sea birds.

Hunter-killers

Killer whales are fierce black and white whales up to about 12 metres long that hunt in packs. Their ivory teeth are strong enough to tear seals and even other whales apart. Sperm whales hunt squid, octopus-like creatures, some almost as big as themselves, that live many hundreds of metres down. Their teeth, only in the lower jaw, are right for clamping and crushing soft, slippery prey.

Small whales

Dolphins and porpoises are the smallest whales, some less than two metres long. They occur all over the world, especially in temperate and cold seas but also in the tropics. Most of them have full rows of needle-sharp teeth that help them to catch and eat fish.

Whales and porpoises navigate by sound. They produce squeaks and groans that travel through the water and echo back from rocks and sandbanks, helping the whales to find their way about. The sounds echo off fish as well, so they too help whales to find their prey.

▲ Dolphins are often friendly animals that play together and swim close to boats. The 'blow-hole' on the top of their head is a nostril for breathing.

Warm Seas

Though comfortable for us to swim in, warm seas are often short of dissolved gases like oxygen on which life depends, and minerals. So warm seas are poor in plant life. This means that fish, seabirds and all the other marine animals are likely to be scarce too. Tropical seas do not have the wealth and variety of life that you find in cooler seas. One important exception is the coral reef, often teeming with life.

Currents

Other exceptions occur where currents of cold water well up. This happens, for example, off the west coasts of southern Africa and South America. There, offshore winds blow surface waters far out to sea. Oxygen and minerals are brought to the top, plankton flourishes, fish multiply, and whales, seals and seabirds gather by the thousand to feed.

The same thing often happens around islands in warm seas. The swirling movement of water caused by currents brings cold water to the surface. The currents provide patches of food for tropical seabirds.

The sea turtle lays 50–100 eggs, buried in the sand above the high tide mark. The eggs are like soft ping-pong balls and take 2–3 months to hatch. No bigger than matchboxes, the little turtles dig themselves out of the sand and race down to the surf, to begin their lives at sea. ▼

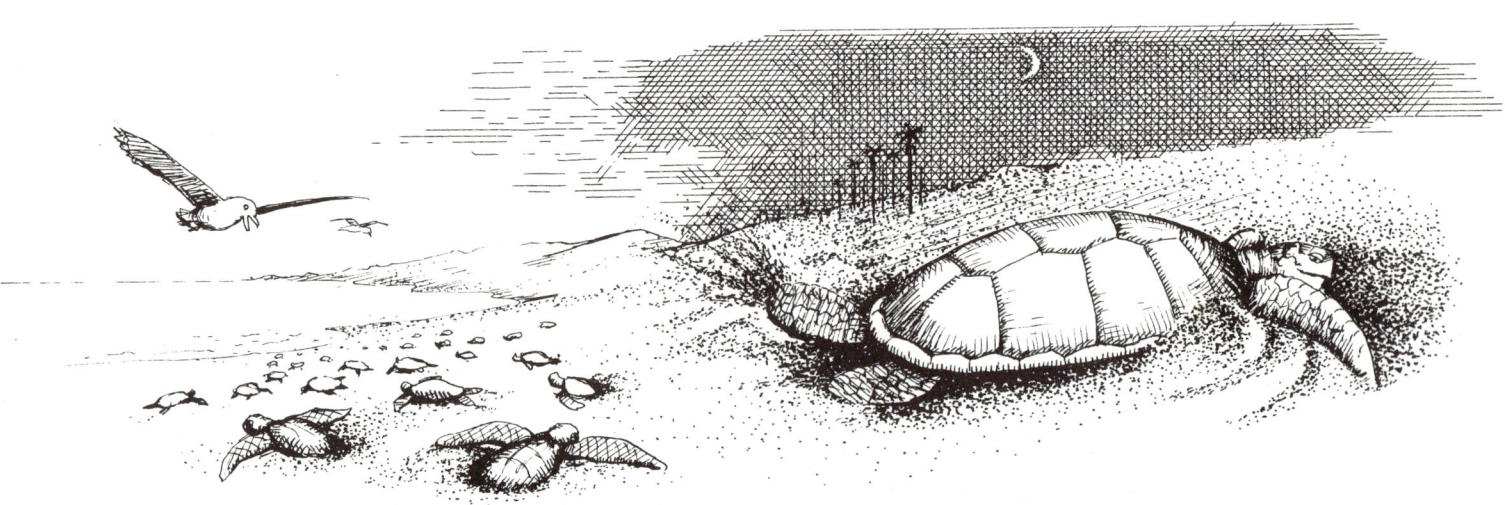

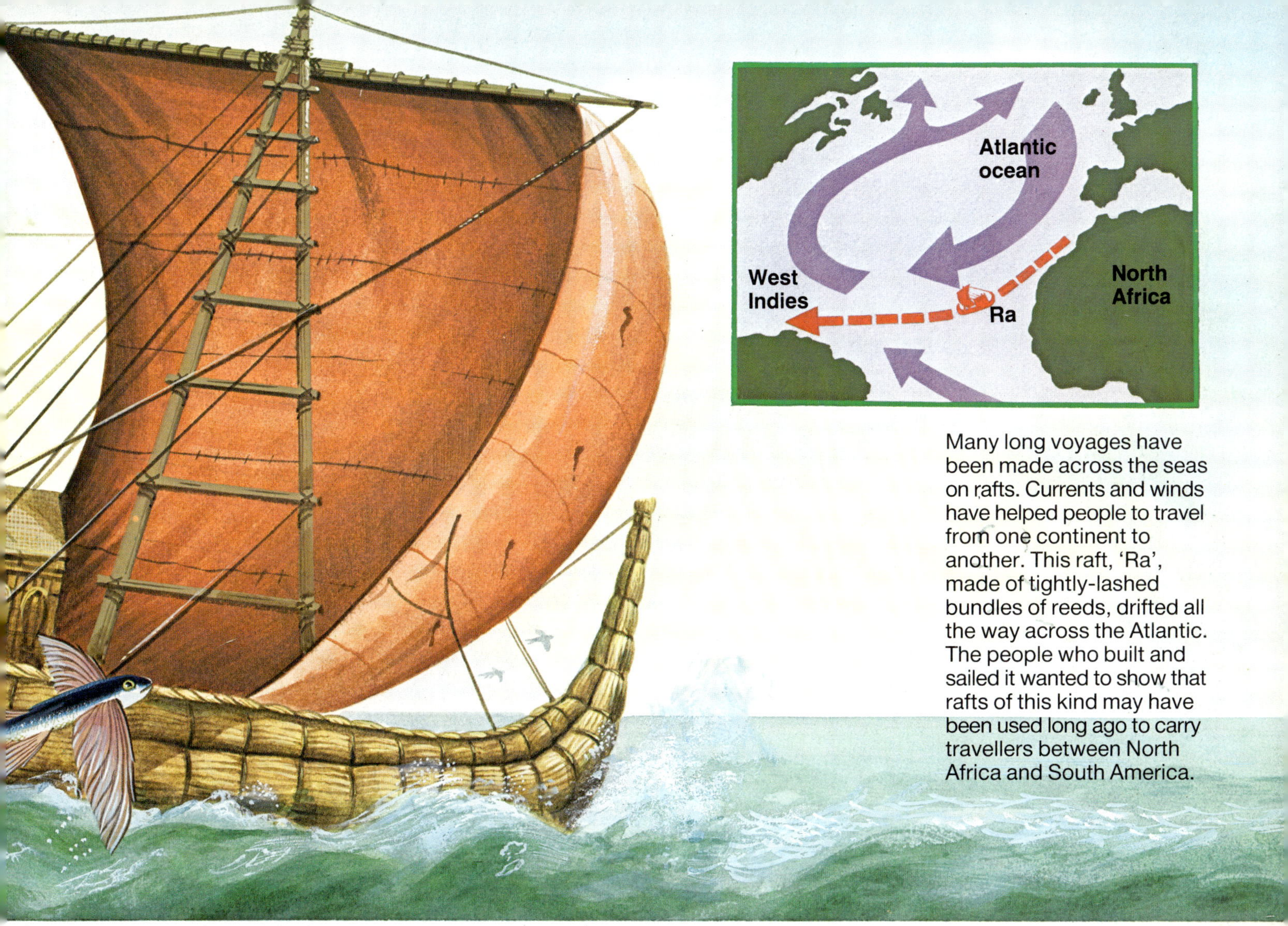

Many long voyages have been made across the seas on rafts. Currents and winds have helped people to travel from one continent to another. This raft, 'Ra', made of tightly-lashed bundles of reeds, drifted all the way across the Atlantic. The people who built and sailed it wanted to show that rafts of this kind may have been used long ago to carry travellers between North Africa and South America.

Currents also bring food for frigate birds and noddies which breed in flocks on the nearby islands. Pacific islanders out fishing in their canoes can always tell where the nearest land lies. They watch the seabirds flying home in the evening, and head the same way themselves.

Drifting with the currents

Crossing a big ocean slowly in a yacht or raft brings you into very close contact with the sea and its animals. Flying fish skim across the bow, sharks and dolphins bump you from underneath, seabirds ride on the masthead and the sea washes over the decks, leaving jellyfish and crabs in the scuppers.

After dark, fish, squid and some larger plankton animals come up from the deep. Some flash brightly with green and yellow lights. On calm nights tropical seas sometimes seem to catch fire as thousands of tiny creatures light up all around.

▲ Sharks are especially active in warm seas. They feed mainly on other fish, but will sometimes attack people as well.

Albatross

Polar Seas

Polar seas are cold seas, covered with drifting sheets of floating ice or ice floes, and dotted with towering icebergs. Floes form on the sea when the surface freezes in autumn. Icebergs are fragments, sometimes huge fragments many kilometres long and deep, that have fallen from land glaciers into the sea.

Floes and bergs drift far from where they were formed, cooling the air and sea around them, eventually melting as they drift into warmer water. Seals and penguins ride them, and whales sometimes come up to scratch their backs on them.

The Arctic Ocean
In the far north, ice-covered ocean extends right to the pole. Around the pole itself the floes are several years old and many metres thick, and there is not much life in the sea between them. Nearer the edges of this pack-ice there is more open water, especially during the summer. When the sun penetrates the icy sea, plankton grows densely and seals, seabirds and whales gather in these oases of plenty.

These king penguins swim in cold seas and nest in colonies of several thousands. Penguins use their wings for swimming instead of flying. ▼

Iceberg

Killer whale

Walruses and other kinds of seal feed entirely at sea. Some spend their whole lives on the pack ice, diving into the water when they are hungry and sleeping off their fishy or plankton meals on the floes. Walruses use their great tusks to scrape clams (shell-fish) from the sea bed. Whales, both the plankton-feeders and the killer whales that prey on them, migrate north from warmer seas to spend their summers in the Arctic. In spring and summer polar bears move out from the land to hunt for seals on the ice. Men hunt seals too for their silky coats.

The Antarctic

The southern polar region is a great ice-covered continent surrounded by sea, with pack-ice extending many kilometres out from the shore. This too is a lively area in summer, when growing plankton turns the water into a greeny-brown soup. Whales and seals are plentiful, just as they are on the Arctic fringe. The whales are the same species (though of separate stocks that never meet their northern cousins). The seals are different species, though no less fat and sleepy. Northern and southern seabirds too are of different species. Over 40 different kinds of birds feed among the Antarctic pack ice, including several species of penguins, terns and graceful albatrosses.

Krill are small shrimp-like animals that live in huge shoals in Antarctic seas, even far south among the ice floes. They are the food of filter-feeding (or baleen) whales, fish, and sea birds such as penguins and albatrosses. ▼

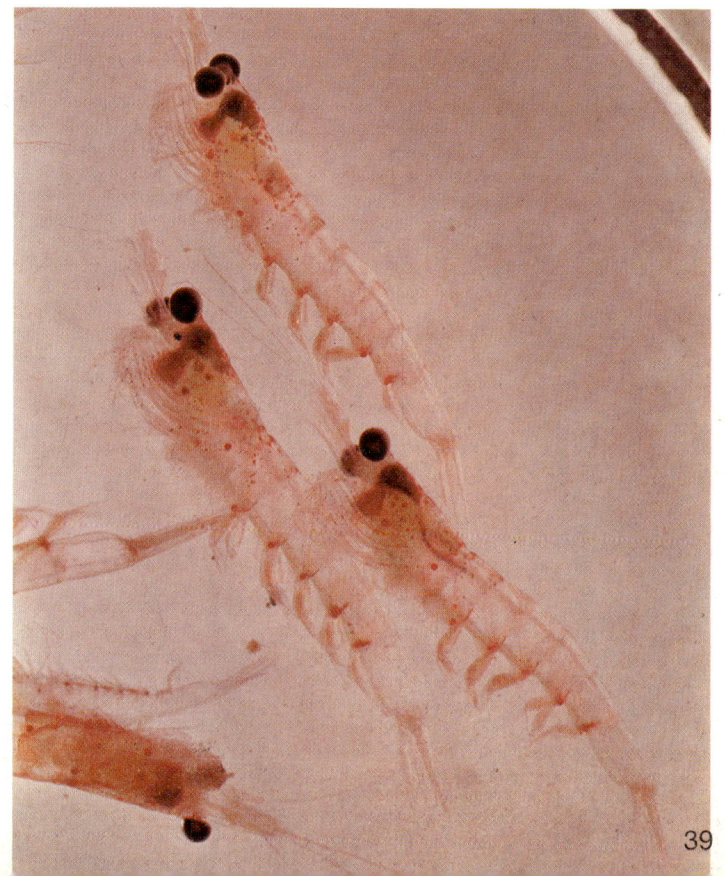

Marine Research

Life in the sea has always been interesting and important to researchers called marine biologists. They have tried to find out what plants and animals live there, how they live, how many there are, and what controls their populations. During the last few years it has become important to us all, for the sea is a source of food and raw materials. It is also the sink into which we pour all our sewage and waste materials from industry. Sooner or later everything ends up in the sea, and many of our waste industrial products are poisoning it. The sea is very big and will take a lot of rubbish, but damage has been done locally for many years, and some people fear its effects are spreading.

HMS *Challenger* explored the world's oceans from 1872 to 1876. Though poorly equipped by modern standards, her scientists and crew brought back many specimens and much information. ▶

This miniature submarine, about to be lowered over the stern of a research ship, sledges over the sea bed, driven by a propeller.

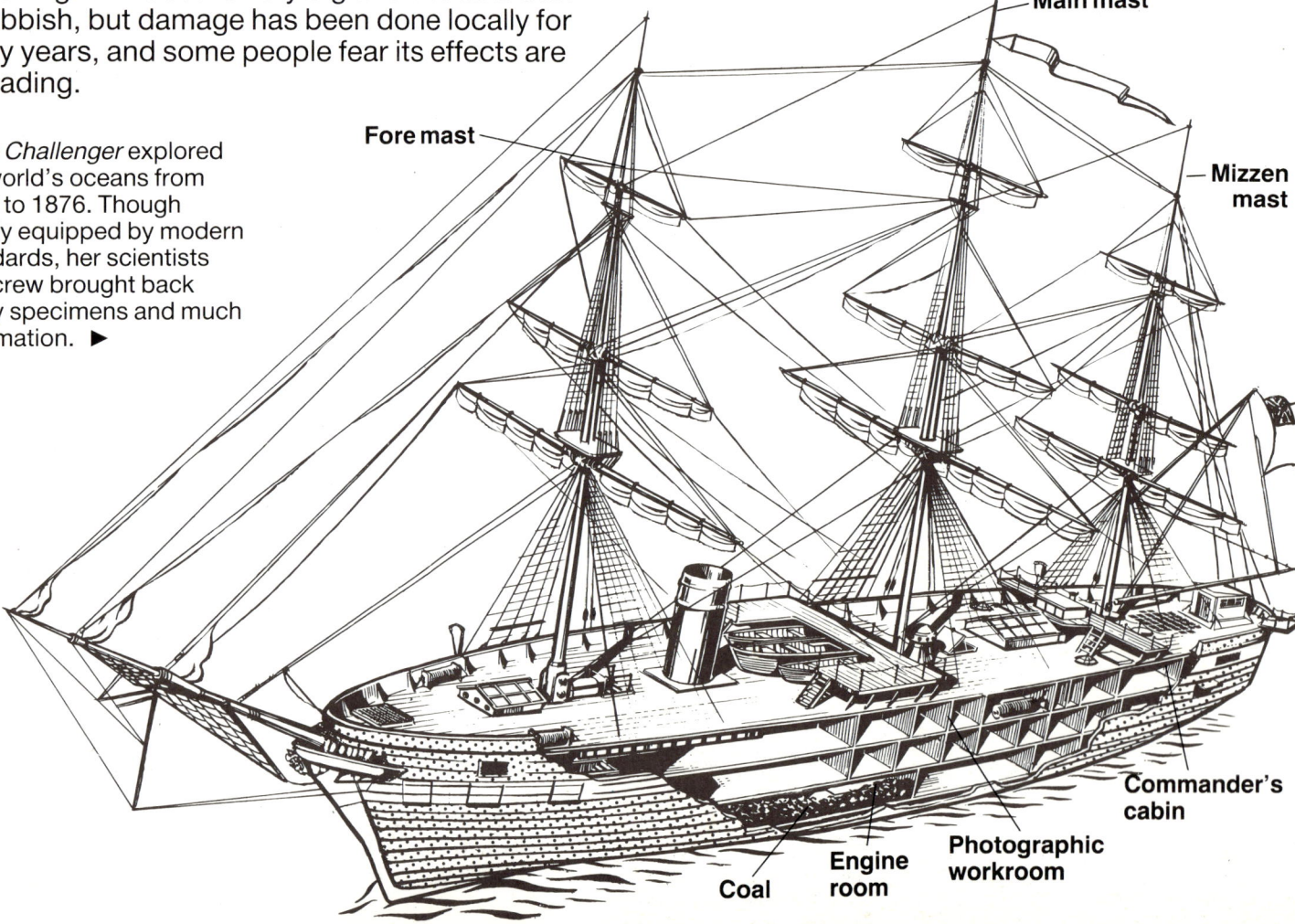

Fore mast

Main mast

Mizzen mast

Commander's cabin

Photographic workroom

Engine room

Coal

This fine nylon net, towed through surface waters, collects plankton for the scientists to examine and identify.

The apparatus in this cage is lowered into the sea and used to measure the temperature and saltiness of the sea at great depths.

HMS Challenger

One of the earliest ships to explore the ocean depths was HMS *Challenger*, which sailed from Britain over 100 years ago. Its main purpose was to explore the ocean bed so that submarine telegraph cable could be laid. But its crew and scientists also discovered a great deal about marine life. Soundings had to be taken with weighted lines. It took many hours to raise and lower the trawl nets with the primitive equipment available on deck, and the scientific apparatus was simple and often unreliable.

Modern survey ships

Modern marine biologists have many advantages and better research conditions than in the past. They work from well-equipped ships in the different seas and oceans of the world. So today we are gathering knowledge of the sea and marine life far more quickly than ever before. If we use the knowledge sensibly we can avoid such dangers as over-fishing and pollution damage, and keep the seas safer for the future.

◀ Royal Research Ship *Bransfield*, a modern vessel working in the Antarctic. Much of its research is on krill. Today's survey ships are safe, fast and efficient. They are equipped with radio and use modern ways of measuring temperature, salinity and depth.

Books and Places

Books to read
Collins Pocket Guide to the Seashore, Barnett, J., Yonge, C. M., Collins, 1958.
A Closer Look at the Oceans, Cook, D. and S., Hamilton, 1976.
The Sea, Engel, L., Time-Life, 1977.
Basic Marine Biology, Fincham, A. A., British Museum (N.H.) C.U.P., 1984.
The Atlantic, Hargreaves, P. Wayland, 1980.
The Pacific, Hargreaves, P., Wayland, 1981.
The Indian Ocean, Hargreaves, P., Wayland, 1981.
The Ocean World, Ryan, P., Penguin, 1973.
A Closer Look at Whales and Dolphins, Stonehouse, B., Hamilton, 1978.
The Living World of the Sea, Stonehouse, B., Hamlyn, 1979.

Places to visit
The shore — Visit as many different kinds of shores as you can — rocky, sandy, muddy, sheltered, exposed, estuaries. Look into rock pools and under stones. Dig in the sand or mud, identify as many kinds of animal and plant as you can. Mark out the different levels of the tides as they go down. How long are different parts of the shore exposed? What kinds of seabird are there? Where are they feeding?

Inshore waters — if you are in a boat, observe the sea: how does the water change as you get away from the shore? Look out for seals, dolphins and different kinds of seabirds.

On shore, take a fishing line and see what you catch among rocks, or on a sandy or muddy sea bed. Try towing a stocking net for ten minutes. Tip your catch into a jar and examine it through a hand-lens or microscope.

Harbours — Fishing ports can be very interesting, especially when the boats are bringing their catches in. Look at the boats and see if you can work out what gear they are using (trawls, lines, seine or drift nets, lobster pots, crab pots). Ask the fishermen how far away they fish and what methods they use. Look at the catches being unloaded and lined up for sale on the docks. What kinds of fish can you identify?

In the depths of the coral reefs lives the lionfish. It attacks and defends itself by jabbing its victims with its deadly spines. ▶

Fishmongers — See how many different kinds of fish you can spot in a fishmonger's; many of them have pictures of fish on their walls, to help identification. If he is not busy, ask him to show you some of the different kinds of fish. Look out for flatfish, eels, crabs, gurnard, squid, lobsters, oysters, cockles, etc.

Museums — Many museums in coastal towns and the Natural History Museum in London, have exhibits about the sea and shore, or about the fishing industry, boats, seabirds, whales and other things to be found by the sea.

Oceanaria — Ports and seaside resorts sometimes have aquaria where you can see fish and other marine creatures alive. You may even be able to see dolphins and porpoises performing. Some of the big zoos, like London's, have aquaria with fish, turtles etc.

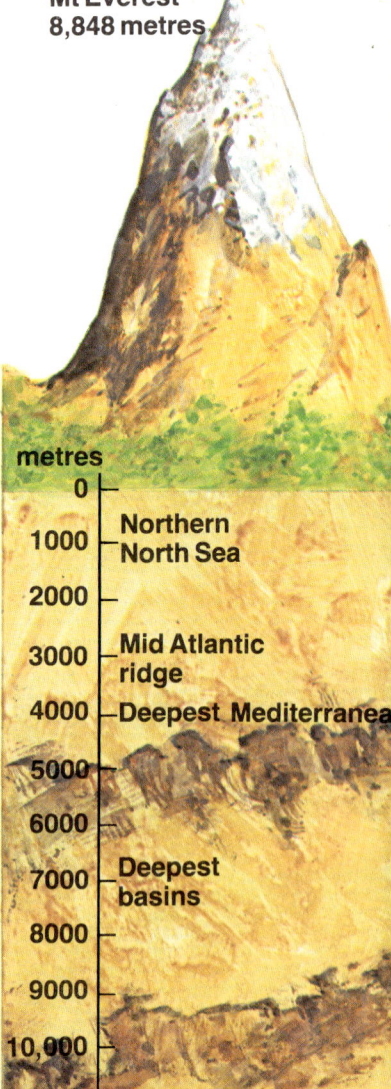

Mt Everest
8,848 metres

metres
0

1000 — Northern North Sea

2000

3000 — Mid Atlantic ridge

4000 — Deepest Mediterranea

5000

6000

7000 — Deepest basins

8000

9000

10,000

Great Explorations

Since the days of steamships most marine exploration and survey has been done by the great navies of the world, especially the British, American, French and German navies. They have special units which explore the oceans continuously and keep charts up-to-date.

Fishermen and fisheries research vessels have also added a lot to our knowledge of the sea, and many universities and other research institutions have their own research ships that operate all over the world. SY *Calypso* is one such research ship, belonging to Jacques Cousteau. It has been especially fitted out for divers and underwater photography.

Exploring the Sea

1768—71 HMS *Endeavour* explored huge unmapped areas of the southern oceans, searching for the unmapped southern continent, Antarctica. Her captain, James Cook, and scientists brought back many valuable specimens, drawings and paintings of marine birds, mammals and other creatures from the south seas.

1772—75 HMS *Resolution* also commanded by Captain James Cook, explored the southern Pacific and Atlantic Oceans even more thoroughly, and came almost within sight of Antarctica through the pack ice.

1826—29 *Astrolabe*, a French naval ship, explored the Pacific Ocean.

1826—30 HMS *Adventure* and HMS *Beagle* worked the Atlantic coast of South America. HMS *Beagle* carried Charles Darwin, who later became famous as the founder of a theory of how plants and animals evolve.

1872—76 HMS *Challenger* was the first ship that set out to explore the depths of the sea. She travelled all the major oceans taking soundings wherever possible, measuring sea temperatures, and collecting specimens from all depths. In the same period a German ship, SMS *Gazelle* explored the southern oceans, whilst the American USS *Tuscarora* also explored the northern seas.

1934 William Beebe descended over 850 metres in a 'bathysphere' or specially strengthened steel ball.

1979 *Alvin*, a deep-water submarine, took scientists to the deep sea bed to take photographs and collect samples.

▲ King Ferdinand and Queen Isabella encouraged Spanish exploration in the 15th century. Here they wave goodbye to ships setting off to the West Indies.

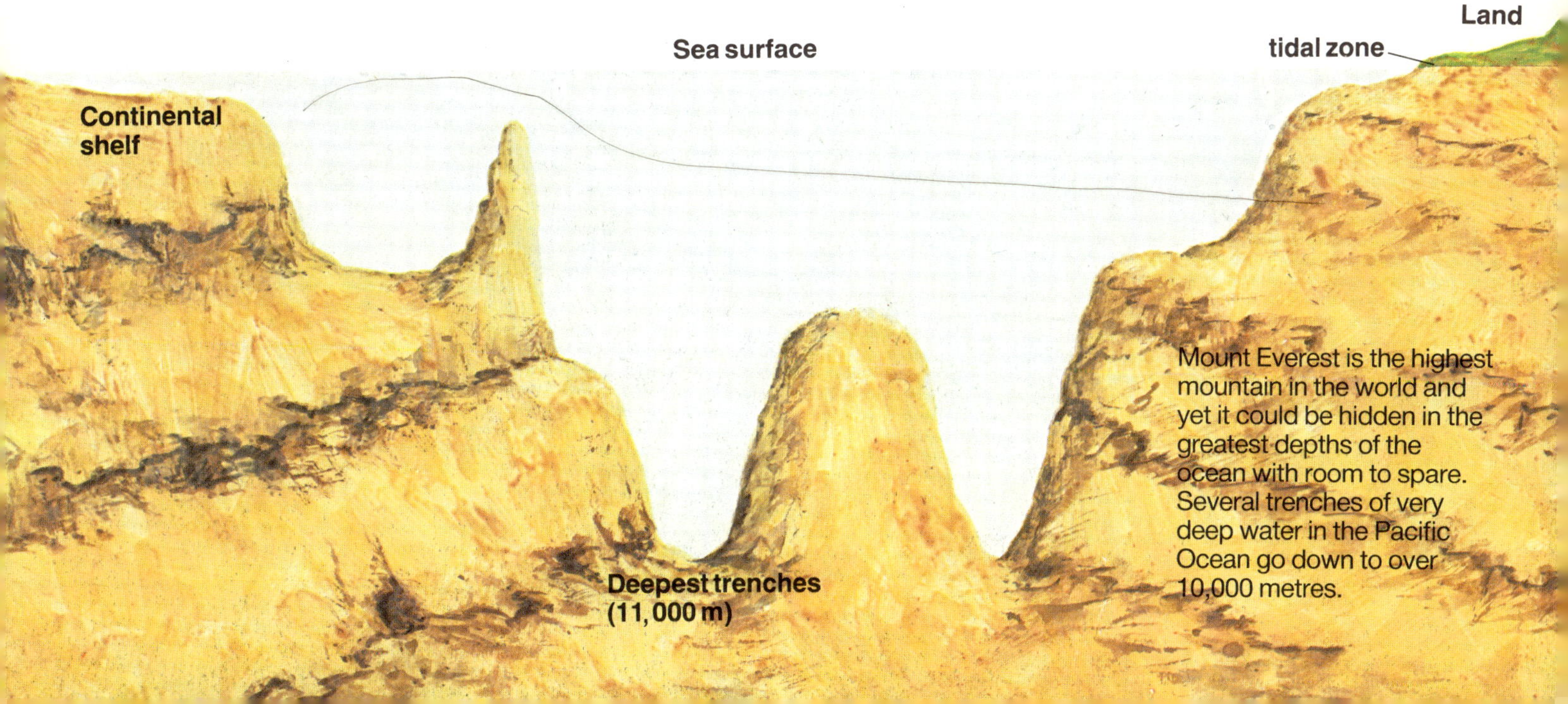

Sea surface

Land

tidal zone

Continental shelf

Deepest trenches (11,000 m)

Mount Everest is the highest mountain in the world and yet it could be hidden in the greatest depths of the ocean with room to spare. Several trenches of very deep water in the Pacific Ocean go down to over 10,000 metres.

Word list

Algae Large group of simple plants, including seaweeds. It is divided into groups by colour: brown algae include bladderwrack, serrated wrack, channelled wrack, and green algae include sea lettuce.

Baleen Horny material forming the filter in a whale's mouth (also called whalebone).

Carnivore Meat-eater.

Currents Great rivers of sea water driven along by wind on the surface or flowing deep below the surface.

Debris Minute particles of dead plants and animals.

Diatom Microscopic plant cell found in surface waters and on the shore.

Erosion Breaking down and wearing away of rocks and soil.

Filter feeding Feeding by straining plankton and debris from the sea water.

Frond Leaf-like part of seaweed.

Glacier Slow-moving mass of ice which eventually melts or breaks up into icebergs.

Habitat Natural surroundings in which a plant or animal lives.

Herbivore Plant-eating animal.

Hold-fast Leathery, root-like structure by which seaweed attaches itself to rock.

Intertidal zone The part of the shore between the high tide mark and the low tide mark which is covered and uncovered by the tide twice a day.

Kelp Long stranded seaweed.

Krill Shrimp-like animals of the zooplankton.

Larva An early stage of development for many young animals.

Lichen Small plant that is made up of both fungal and algal cells.

Nutrients Substances in sea water that provide food for plants and animals.

Oarweed Type of seaweed, with strands 10 or more metres long, similar to kelp.

Organism Living animal or plant.

Pack-ice Broken-up sheet of ice on surface of sea or lake.

Phytoplankton Plants of the plankton.

Plankton Plants and animals that drift in surface waters.

Polyp Small soft-bodied animals forming the living part of coral reefs.

Predator Animal which kills other animals for food; a hunting animal.

Reef Rocky mass in shallow water.

Salinity Saltiness

Scuppers Drainage holes in the side of a ship.

Sediment Sand, mud or other fine particles deposited in water.

Shoal Group of fish.

Species Type, or kind of plant or animal.

Soundings Measuring the depth of water.

Tentacle Arm-like part of an animal which is used for feeling and grasping and often for catching food.

Waders Birds that find their food in the sand or mud at the edge of shallow waters.

Wrack Type of seaweed. (See different wrack illustrated on page 17.)

Zooplankton Animals of the plankton.

Index

Illustrations appear in **bold** type.

Albatross **38**, 39
Algae **18**, **19**, 44
Alvin 11, **11**, 43
Anchovies 27
Antarctic 39, **39**, **41**
Antarctica 24, 43
Arctic Ocean 38
Arrow worms 27
Atlantic Ocean 8, 24, 32, **37**, 43

Barnacles 13, 18, **18**, 19
Bathysphere 43
Beebe, William 43
Bladder wrack **12**, **17**, 44
Blue grunts **22**
Brill 31

Caspian Sea 8
Carnivorous animals 26, 27
Clams **21**, 23, 38
Channelled wrack **17**, 44
Cockles 20, 21, **21**, 42
Cod 31, 32
Cook, James 43
Coral reef **11**, 22–23, **22**, **23**, 28, **42**
Cousteau, Jacques 43
Crabs 18, **18**, 19, **20**, **21**, 27, **30**, 31, 37, 42
Curlew 21
Currents 24, **24**, 36, **37**, 44

Darwin, Charles 43
Diatom 16, 18, 21, 26, 44
Dog whelks 18
Dolphins **9**, 28, 34, **34**, 35, **35**, 37, 42
Drift nets 33, **33**, 42
Drifters 27

Dunlin 21

Eels 28, 42

Fan worms 21
Filter feeding animals 31, 44
Flat fish 42
Flying fish **9**, **29**, 37
Frigate birds 37
Fulmars 27

Gannet **27**
Great Barrier Reef 22
Gurnard **31**, 42
Gulf Stream 24

Haddock **29**, 33
Hake 33
Herbivorous animals 26, 27
Herrings 27, **28**, 33
High tide mark 12, 16, **17**, 44
HMS Challenger **40**, 41, 43
Hold fasts 16, **16**, 19, 44

Icebergs 38, 44
Ice-floes 39, 44
Inshore waters 42
Intertidal zone 12, 44

Jellyfish 27, 37

Kelp 16, 30, 44
Krill 27, **39**, 41, 44

Limpets 15, 18, 19, **19**
Lionfish **42**
Lobsters **30**, 31, 42
Low tide 12, **14**, 16, **16**, **17**, 23, 30, 44
Lug-worms 20, 21, **21**

Mackerel **29**, 32
Manta ray 28, **29**

Marlin 28
Moray eels 23
Mussels 18, 21, 27

Noddies 37
North Sea 32
Nutrients 24, 26, 44

Oarweed 16, **17**, 30, 44
Off-shore winds 36
Oxygen 21, 24, 36
Oysters 21, 42
Oyster-catcher 21

Pacific Ocean 8, **24**, 32, 43, **43**
Pack-ice 38, 39, 43, 44
Peacock worm **20**
Penguins 27, 38, **38**, **39**
Periwinkle snails **13**, 18, 19, **21**
Plaice **30**, 31
Plankton **26**, 27, 28, **35**, 36, 38, **41**, 44
   phytoplankton 27, 44
   zooplankton **26**, 27, 44
Polar bears 39
Polyps 22, **22**, 44
Porpoise 34, 42
Prawns 18

Ra **37**
Rag worms **20**, 21
Razor shells 20, 21
Red Sea 8
Red shank 21
Research ships **41**, 43
   see also survey ships
Rocks 8, 13, **13**, 15, 16, 18, 20, 44
Rock pools 18, **18**, 42

Saithe 31

Salmon 33
Sea anemones 18, **18**, 22, 27
Sea bed 30, **30**, 33, **33**, 42, 43
Sea-urchins 18, **19**, 23, **30** 31
Seals **34**, 35, 36, 38
Seaweeds 10, 12, 15, **15**, 16–17, **16**, **17**, 18, 19, 20, 30, 44
Seine nets 33, **33**, 42
Serrated wrack **12**, **17**, 44
Sharks 27, **28**, 29, 37, **37**
Shellfish 21, 22, 27, **30**, 31
Shore 10, 12, 15, **15**, 16, **17**, 18, 19, 42
Spiral wrack **17**
Sponges 22, 23, 27, 31
Squid 31, 35, 37, 42
Starfish 18, **19**, **22**, 27, **30**, 31
Storm petrels 27
Submarines 11, **11**, **40**, 43
Sun-fish 28, **29**
Surface waters 24, **24**, 36, 44
Survey ships 41, **41**

Tentacles 18, **20**, 21, 27, 44
Tides 10, 12–13, 15, 18, 42, 44
   spring tides 12
Trade winds 24
Trawl net 33, **33**, 41, 42
Trout 33
Tuna 28
Turtle **36**

Walruses 39
Whales 11, 27, **34**, 34–35, **35**, 36, 38, **39**, 42, 44
White Sea 8